Waves are Wet

And Other Short Stories

By April McMurtrey with Chantel McCabe
Edited by Megan Hambly

*For use with lessons 31-40
in the Learn Reading program*

Copyright 2019 by April McMurtrey
Printed in the United States of America

Learn Reading
3717 Acadia Circle
Bakersfield, CA 93311

Visit us at: LearnReading.com

All rights reserved. No portion of this publication may be reproduced by any means, including duplicating, photocopying, electronic, mechanical, recording, the World Wide Web, e-mail, or otherwise, without written permission from Learn Reading.

V.1.1.

ISBN# 9781660262861

Contents:

Lesson 31..5

Lesson 32..13

Lesson 33..21

Lesson 34..29

Lesson 35..37

Lesson 36..45

Lesson 37..53

Lesson 38..61

Lesson 39..69

Lesson 40..77

LESSON 31

Wade and Webster

Wade and Webster were on vacation. They were twins. "Wake up, Webster! It is past twelve!" insisted Wade.

"I am awake!" said Webster.

"Well, get up! Don't dwell in bed!" Wade demanded.

"I am on vacation!"

"Well, it is silly to spend your vacation in bed! The waves and swells are splendid. There is no wind," said Wade.

"Wade can't wade in the waves!" Webster said in a nasty tone.

"Webster, you are so silly! You are not witty! I told Dad you are still in bed and he is mad!" said Wade.

"You told Dad? You are a pesty telltale, Wade!" said a cross Webster.

Waves are Wet

Webster and Wade went for a swim. They left Dad to bake in the sun on the sand.

"Beware of the rips and drift! The waves can be swift!" Dad said.

"It is windy and wet!" said Webster sadly.

"Well, waves are wet, Webster! It is fun if you get in!" said Wade.

"Wade gets to wade!" Webster said in that nasty tone.

"Webster, don't be silly! If you get in, you could be the winner! Last one in is a smelly hog!" Wade said.

Webster got in fast and insisted, "I am the winner! You are a smelly hog!"

"Silly Webster! He fell for it!" said Wade with a giggle. The lads swam and swam. They bobbed in the wake of a vessel. It was fantastic.

Wafers for Webster

"I felt a nip on my leg!" Webster insisted.

"It could be a mullet that bit you! I saw some in the swells!" said Wade.

Webster went to Dad and said, "My leg is swollen. A mullet bit me!"

"Let me inspect your leg, Webster," said Dad as Webster wept. "It isn't bad. Don't dwell on it! Go get a wafer from the store."

The lads went to the store to get wafers. They spotted a scantily clad lass by Dad.

After they got the wafers, Wade demanded, "Who was that? Was that Wendy?"

"Was that a possible wife?" Webster said.

"No!" said Dad. "I am not on vacation to get a wife! That was a random person that lost her hat in the wind."

Wade said, "Dad, you are red. A lot of sun can be bad for the welfare of your skin!"

A Dad Webcast

The wind came up from the west. It got dim and cold. It felt like winter. "Let's get to the cabin!" Dad said. The crosswind swept up the sand and it hit their bare legs. They ran to the cabin as fast as they could.

Dad lit the lantern and put on the kettle. "I plan to hop on the bandwagon and do a webcast," said Dad. "I got the software for my computer. Can you help me set it up after dinner, twins?"

"A dad webcast!" said Wade. "It will do well!"

"Can I be your webmaster, Dad? I am the best at computers!" said Webster.

Wedges for Dinner

"Dad, can you make wedges of cod for dinner? I want twenty!" said Webster.

"Twenty? That is a lot of cod! Will twelve do?" said Dad.

"Only twelve?" said Webster. "I am a cold and hungry lad!"

"I will add pumpkin and salad. It will be a swell dinner!" said Dad.

"Can you bake us a cake?" said Wade.

"Yes; but you two had better help me so dinner can be swift. We have webcast tasks to do," said Dad.

Dad made the cake and the cod wedges. Webster cut the pumpkin and Wade made the salad.

"Dinner was a winner!" the twins told their dad.

LESSON 32

A Little Wind

"We are on vacation! Let's go for a bike ride!" said Dad.

"No," said Webster. "It wouldn't be wise. The wind is icy! It would be better to drive."

"You can put on your hat and mittens!" said Dad.

"Would our bike ride be a mile or two? Or five or nine?" said Wade.

"Only five miles!" said Dad. "It is a little trip, but we can observe and be close to the environment."

"I propose we sit here and take time to set up Dad's website and online store!" said Webster.

"Online store? I do not intend to sell!" insisted Dad.

"Dad! If you have a webcast, you must sell items!" insisted Webster.

"Webster, my advice is that we do online tasks after dinner. We can't hide in the cabin from a little wind! Let's take the time to ride side by side. It is not like the website is a crisis!" said Dad.

A Vacation Bike Ride

Dad and the twins set off on their bike ride in their hats and mittens. "It is like ice!" Webster insisted.

After a mile, they rode up a rise.

"My legs are sore! It isn't nice!" Webster insisted. They stop to rest at the top of the rise and spot kittens that hunt mice.

"That is rad! This ride in the environment isn't that bad!" Webster admitted.

They rode for a mile to a picnic site. "It is fine to dine midst the vines and pines," said Wade. "We could make an advertisement for Dad's webcast on this trip!"

"Dad, do you have an agenda for your webcast and site?" Webster said.

"My webcast agenda is life!" said Dad.

"Life? I like it!" said Wade.

The Silver Mine

The lads rode their bikes past a silver mine. They stop to spot life on the mine site. They spot tiny, distant men on the mine. "The mine is so wide! They must drive to that place. Is there a pile of silver we can take?" said Webster.

"No," said Dad. "The silver is the mine's! It Is not for us. Do not step past that wire."

"Let's get back to the cabin as Webster could make a crisis," said Wade. "If Webster stole some silver, we could end up in prison!"

"You are so wise, Wade. That is wise advice. Let's go past the mine fast!" said Dad.

"You two are vile!" Webster insisted. "I'm not so daft!"

A Fast Ride to the Cabin

For the last mile, they rode twice as fast because they were hungry. They went past the side of an old temple site. Dad said, "That is a holy site. You go to admit your vices and be a better person."

"I have no vices because I am a sensible person," said Webster.

"It is improbable that you are sensible. I am the wise one!" said Wade.

"Let's get to the cabin fast. We must put on some rice for dinner and set up my website!" said Dad. The lads sped to the cabin. They had had a fine time on their bike ride.

Dad's Plan

Dinner was simple but decent.

"Dad, smile!" said Wade. "I must take a shot of you for your website!"

"No," said Dad, "that would be a crisis! I am a mess. I must be at my best for that shot!"

"If Dad plans to get a wife because of his webcast, he must smile and not be in a dire mess," Webster said.

"My plan isn't to get a wife!" said Dad.

"Dad protests a lot!" said Webster.

"My plan is to do presentations on life! I am not on the hunt for a wife!" Dad insisted.

"Let Dad be, Webster. Dad has a fine plan for his website. Don't be a pest and hassle him," said Wade.

LESSON 33

The Art Market

Mark and Barb started a little store at the art market in Boston. Mark was an artist and Barb was a yarn fanatic. Bart, from the local TV station, did a presentation on their store. "It started when Mark said to me that I could fill a store with my yarn at home. I do have a lot!" Barb giggled.

Mark said, "Barb told me my art is fantastic and that there is a market for it. My art is large and stark."

"We attended a seminar on market store operation in March. It was fantastic," said Barb.

"Yarn and art is an odd combination, but the locals are smitten: yarn snobs and art snobs alike!" said Bart.

Sparky the Smart Car

Mark and Barb had a two-tone smart car. The smart car's name was Sparky. Mark said, "Sparky is nice to park as it is tiny, but it has no space for cargo. Sparky was a splendid start for our store but is not a cargo vessel. We must improvise and get a cart to add to Sparky to hold the yarn and art. It could be possible for us to get a large car if the locals still visit the store endlessly and spend on our yarn and art," Mark observed.

"Bart's TV presentation did help," said Barb. "His presentation made hundreds of locals visit our market store. The locals spent thousands on yarn and art! I felt like a star."

"They come from far and wide. They fill up the car park. We don't have to advertise because of Bart!" said Mark. "Perhaps the locals will still come to buy yarn and art and we can buy a large car!"

Lessons for Locals

Mark sat in the store and carved some art out of bark. It made a bit of a mess. Barb made a start on a scarf. "If we had a farm with a large barn for our art, we could make a lot of items for our store," said Barb.

"To carve in the store is not the best," admitted Mark, "but people are impressed to be able to inspect an artist start some art. That would not be possible on a farm!"

"We could do lessons for locals in the store," said Barb. "The locals like lessons!"

"That could be smart," said Mark. "We could rent that space at the arcade if the lessons get large."

The Harvest Market

Madge and Rod took Coco, the ape, to the harvest market to get her some bananas. "This market has the best items from our local farms," Madge said. "It is smart to take a cart. We must start on one side of the market and fill up the cart."

"Did we come here for a lot of items? My list only has bananas on it!" said an alarmed Rod.

"Rod, you can't come to a splendid harvest market and only get one item!" insisted Madge as she darted off to get some melons and lemons.

"The cart has no space left in it," said Rod. "Can we depart?"

"We must get one more item!" insisted Madge. "I want apples so I can make an apple tart!"

Coco the Ape Model

Madge spotted the art market on the side of the car park and said, "Let's take the cart to the car and go to the art market. Mark and Barb have their store over here."

"Mark and Barb? The art and yarn store that was on TV?" said Rod.

"That's the one! I would like to ask Mark if he can do some art," said Madge.

"Some art? Would Coco be the model?" said Rod. "I would like to get a bit of yarn to add to Coco's nest. Let's go!"

They got to the store and met Mark and Barb in person. "Mark, do you do pet art? I would like Coco to be your model," said Madge.

"I do not do pet art but I could start. There is a large market for that," said Mark.

LESSON 34

Bertha's Diner

"Pet art? I love it! The locals love their pets. Do the math, Mark!" said Barb.

"But I can't make pet art. Rod and Madge have got an ape!" said Mark.

"There are lessons on YouTube, Mark. You can do it! Tell them you can do Coco as a test," said Barb.

"That's a plan!" Mark said. "I'm hungry. Let's get a bite at Bertha's Diner!"

"Bertha's Diner? Isn't that the filthy place at the harvest market?" said Barb.

"No, it isn't filthy. It is a fun, ethnic place. It is a Celtic diner. They make a splendid broth there. Let's go!" said Mark.

They got to the diner and Beth, a Celtic lass, said, "Hi Mark!"

"I gather you met her here?" said Barb.

"The staff and locals at Bertha's Diner spotted me on TV in Bart's presentation for the store. I am like a star! " said Mark.

Celtic Fun

Seth is a bit of a sloth and could do with a bath. He was at the till at the diner and said, "There's Barb and Mark! They were on TV! I love their arts and crafts!"

"This place is a bit odd," said an alarmed Barb. "They have some eccentric items here!"

"It is harmless!" insisted Mark.

"Are you up for some Celtic fun?" said Seth.

"We are here for the broth," said Barb; but Mark was agog for some fun.

"Mark, sit on the throne!" demanded Seth. "Thump on the table to assemble the staff. Give the staff some tasks. Barb, you can act like staff! Take this cloth and mop up that mess!"

"I am not staff! I am entitled to sit!" Barb insists. "Mark!" spat Barb. "This place is demented! Seth is a flake and a thug!"

"Pardon me, Barb, but this is a bit of fun! Mop up the froth and you can have your broth," said Seth.

"It is best if we do it so we can escape!" said Mark. So Mark thumped the table and Barb dabbed the froth on the tiles. They ate their broth as fast as they could and left.

Mark and Barb go Home

"That was odd!" said Mark.

"That place is demented. We must go on Moth Radio and tell our tale!" said Barb. "Let's go home. I must rest in the bathtub. That odd place made my legs throb." Mark and Barb sped home in Sparky, the smart car. Barb got in a hot bath filled with froth and bubbles. Mark settled on the bed with a thriller on TV. There was a thunderclap. The thunder ended Barb's bath suddenly as it would be risky to still be in the bathtub.

"Barb, you are so nimble to rise so fast. I love the thrill of thunder!" Mark said.

The thunder gave me a start," said Barb, "and I want to get to bed. It is pathetic but I would like a thimble of rice for dinner. I must get to bed," said Barb. Mark got Barb a tiny bit of rice, then got himself a decent dinner as he was hungry.

Mark and Barb Take a Rest

"Mark, we must go on a vacation and be sloths for a bit," said Barb. "I have said it thrice that we must take a rest from the store. We could probably go for a bit from the fifth of March. Would that do?"

"I would love that!" said Mark.

"I could make an item or two from this ethically made cloth for the trip. It has the width for a dress," said Barb.

"Could you make a thermal vest for me? It can still be icy in March!" said Mark.

"Yes. And we could get Madge to run the store for us. Madge is ethical and there will be no theft. Madge is the best! We had better tell her to not go to Bertha's Diner. That would not impress her!" giggled Barb.

A Nest for Coco

Madge said she would run the store if she could have a nest for Coco at the till. "I must admit, I love Coco," said Madge. "At first I said Rod was demented to adopt an ape, but she is like a baby! I can't withstand that little nimble lass." Barb told Madge she could have the nest for Coco at the till.

"I have a nice method to run a store splendidly," said Madge.

"That is fantastic!" said Barb.

In their scramble to set off on vacation, they did not tell Madge to not go to Bertha's Diner. Seth stopped by the store and said, "Would you like to come have some broth at Bertha's Diner, Madge?"

"Only if I can take Coco with me!" insisted Madge.

"Coco is an ape, I gather? Fantastic!" giggled Seth.

They entered the diner and could discern the throb of a Celtic anthem. "Decent harmonics!" said Madge.

LESSON 35

Fish with Mash

Madge and Coco sat at a table. Seth sat there, too. "I wish to have one fish with mash for me and one banana for Coco! Do you take cash?" Madge said to Beth.

"Yes," Beth said to Madge. Then Beth stared at Seth and said, "Seth, don't mess with Madge. She is a respected general!" said Beth.

"A general! Generals are sharp and adaptable. This will be fun!" said Seth to Beth.

Beth said. "You have no shame!"

Seth shrugged and demanded, "Madge, you are a noble lass! Sit at the throne to have your fish and mash!"

"I am in a rush. I will have my fish here at the table. Take your hand off me or I will crush it as punishment," said Madge in a sharp and icy tone. And that was that! Madge and Coco ate and left the diner. Seth felt shaky and blushed.

"Madge is truly a general. She has the best attitude. I wish I could be like that!" Beth said to the staff at the bar.

Shelly's Milkshake Store

Rod dashed to the store to assist Madge with a shipment of yarn. "Barb has got a lot of yarn! There is no space for it! It is an impossible task," lamented Madge.

"They must get a larger store!" said Rod. "We must store some of the yarn in the shed."

"Let's go get a milkshake at the market," said Madge. "I am done with this punishment!"

The TV was on at Shelly's milkshake store. A local shrimp fisherman had lost a lot of cash in a shady hush-hush matter with a selfish hotshot. "That makes me cross! They should crush unethical commerce!" insisted Madge with a thump on the table.

Shelly smashed some bananas in a dish for Coco and made vanilla milkshakes for Rod and Madge.

Notions about Nut Milk

"I have no option but to go to my dad's nut farm and make a go of it there," said a feverish Josh on TV with a blush. "My shrimp commerce has been absolutely smashed. I lost my shrimp ship to a selfish man. It is a shame. I wish I had the cash to give it a better shot."

"Nut farms are a truly super option," said Madge to Rod. "Nut milk is in demand! That milkshake of yours is not made out of animal milk, it is made out of nut milk!"

"It is? This milkshake is splendid! That shatters my notions about nut milk!" said Rod.

"I wish to send Josh a letter to give him some sensible advice and tell him to be gentle with himself," said Madge.

Nut Fever

Josh got Madge's letter. He felt better about his life on his dad's nut farm. He sent Madge a letter and said, "Would you like to visit us at the nut farm? It is on a splendid estate with a lodge for visits. There's no rush!"

"Let's do it! We could take Bart from the TV station with us! He is sharp. He could make a shiny promotion for Josh! This would give Josh a shot to make a lot of cash. He could crush it!" gushed Madge.

"You have nut fever, Madge! The nut estate must be lush. I could do with a nice vacation," said Rod with a shrug.

"Don't be selfish. It is not a vacation. We will be there to assist a shaky lad and his dad. You look a mess, Rod. Have a shave and let's get to the farm," insisted Madge.

Ash's Accident

Rod, Madge, Coco, and Bart set off for the nut farm with Ash, the TV intern. They got to the lodge and Ash fell over a sharp spike by the shed. She gashed her leg and felt shaky. "That was a bad start to smash and bash your shin like that!" said Bart.

Josh rushed to the lodge to assist Ash. "That is a shame, Ash. Do you want to rush to the clinic for a shot? I have got the cash," said Josh.

"No," blushed Ash. "I will be fine! It was selfish of me to trip and mess up the visit."

"You were not selfish! It was an accident!" Josh insisted.

Ash felt shattered and a bit feverish. "I must rest," she said.

LESSON 36

Get Ash to the Clinic

"We must get Ash to the clinic fast!" insisted Madge. "Her fever is up, her skin is rosy, and her gash could be ulcerous!"

"That is ominous!" said a nervous Josh.

"I don't want to be pompous or callous, but if you cannot help you must not come to the clinic with us!" said Madge to the men. "It could be perilous for Ash if we mess this up."

"Absolutely!" the men said as one.

In the end, Madge and Josh sped Ash to the clinic. "Isn't Madge fabulous?" said Rod. "She can handle a momentous crisis like this."

"She is marvellous and talented!" said Bart. "The clinic had better make Ash better!"

The Voluminous Clinic Papers

Madge, Josh, and Ash entered the clinic. "Help!" demanded Madge. "We have a risky case over here!"

"Let me inspect her while you fill in the voluminous clinic papers," said the clinic man to Madge.

"They are voluminous and they do not impress me! I cannot fill in numerous spaces as I am not kin," said Madge.

"Are you her cousin?" the man asked Josh.

"No, we met a little time ago," said Josh.

"I think the lad is smitten!" said the man.

"Don't be ludicrous!" said Madge. "He is oblivious to that! He is crushed and unhappy that she is ill and gashed! Inspect the lass as it is an emergency!"

Fill in the Papers

"Josh, get Bart to come here. He must come here to fill in the clinic papers. I shouldn't do it with fictitious information!" said Madge.

"Is Bart her dad?" asked the man.

"No, Bart is her boss. He is a famous TV presenter," said Madge.

"That is fabulous! I have never met a famous TV presenter here in the country!" said the man.

"You are monstrous!" said a thunderous Madge. "Inspect the lass!"

The man was ponderous at last and said, "Well, if you insist. There is some mucous and her skin is luminous. She has a fever that could be infectious. We must put on masks!"

"Infectious fever? But she fell on a spike! This is scandalous. Get your boss!" demanded Madge.

Ash's Inspection

The clinic boss was nervous and said, "That man is not a medical person. He is the most ambitious and pretentious man on our staff. I realize it is contentious but he likes to pretend he is medical staff. His task is to mop the tiles."

Madge was still for a second and said in an icy tone, "If you are a medical person, inspect this lass. It is an emergency!"

"The gash could get infected. She must take some pills for that. Ash must get some rest and have some dinner. She is hungry. She will shake that fever," said the clinic boss.

"That is fabulous!" said Madge.

"I can offer you and Josh some scrumptious cake as it will still be some time till she can go," said the clinic boss.

"That is generous of you," said Madge. "We are hungry, too!"

Bart at the Clinic

Bart entered the clinic at last. "I got lost!" said Bart.

"We have had a bit of a scandal over here, Bart. I will spare you the tale. Have some scrumptious cake and fill in Ash's clinic papers for her," insisted Madge. "The cake is fabulous and Ash is on the mend!"

"Are you Bart, the famous TV presenter?" said the clinic boss. "How marvelous!"

"This is so repetitious," said Madge. "This is that same Bart!"

"My wife is a fan," said the clinic boss. "She has a monstrous crush on you, Bart."

"How nice!" giggled nervous Bart.

"Can we go to the lodge? I want to be with Rod and Coco. That would be fabulous," said Madge.

LESSON 37

Ash Has Fun

The men were going to go inspect the nut farm. Ash had been resting at the lodge. She was a lot better. "I am done resting, Madge. I would like to have some fun!" insisted Ash.

"Coco and I are having a go at bingo. You could have a go, too. Bingo with an ape is odd. You have to improvise!" said Madge.

"That could be interesting!" giggled Ash.

Coco flung the bingo set on the tiles with a bang. "She is hungry. I must cut some mango up for her," said Madge.

"Can we have a go at Ping-Pong™ when Coco is done with her mango? They have a Ping Pong™ table over there," said Ash.

"Ping-Pong™ makes Coco angry. The little ball is so maddening for her. It makes her swing madly at it," said Madge.

"That could be alarming!" said Ash.

Ape Lingo

Coco ate her cut-up mango off a plate. Ash spotted a bongo on a table.

"Can Coco bang on a bongo?" said Ash.

"Coco can thump a bongo like a pro!" said Madge.

"She can?"

"She is talented and got the hang of it. She banged on the bongo and I sang. It was fantastic!" said Madge.

"I am so happy you could bring Coco along on this trip! She is an engaging little animal," said Ash.

"Coco is the best thing to happen to me, but it is a huge task to have an ape. I even have to use ape lingo!" said Madge.

"Ape lingo is a thing?" said Ash.

"You bet!" said Madge. "It is interesting to be able to use it."

Coco's Bongo Thumps

Madge and Ash sang to Coco's bongo thumps. The men got back to the lodge and spotted their little concert.

"They are so engaging! I am smitten!" said Rod.

"Me too!" said Bart and Josh.

Rod stared at the men with alarm and said, "That's interesting!"

Josh was bopping along to the song. "I am so happy that I'm not living on a smelly shrimp ship!" said Josh. "Life on the nut farm is the best!"

"The men are back!" said Madge. "Did you like our little song?"

"We did! Madge, there is a harvest dinner dance at the hotel. Josh's dad said we should go," said Rod.

"Including Coco?" said Madge.

"Including Coco!" said Josh.

"That is generous. I have emergency dresses in my tote for the two of us!" said Madge.

The Harvest Dinner Dance

The gang from the nut farm went to the hotel to attend the harvest dinner dance.

"Did you bring along King Kong?" said a silly man who had spotted Coco.

"That is ludicrous. King Kong doesn't have a dress!" insisted Madge.

"Can I have a dance with her?" said the silly man in a provoking manner.

"No! Coco is not here for your amusement," said an angry Madge.

"That is a maddening little man!" Madge said to Ash. "I didn't bring Coco here for that!"

"Let's get going. We can't get along with everyone!" said Ash.

"Oh no! Coco has spotted the band's bongo!" said Madge. "I must distract her with some mango!"

Talented Coco

It was too late. Coco had spotted the bongo on the bandstand and there was no stopping her. She crept up some rungs and hid in the wings of the stage.

"This is going to be interesting!" said Rod.

"It could be splendid advertising for ape liberation if she behaves," said Madge.

"Ash! Let us distract the band and do a fantastic tango!" insisted Josh.

With Ash and Josh distracting the band, Coco was able to get to the bongo undetected. She gave it a little tap. After that, she tapped it twice. She gave it a bang and then a thump. It felt fantastic! She started thumping along with the band. Coco was a talented ape!

LESSON 38

The Tango Ends

"This is so festive! It is like being on the set of Animal Kingdom!" said an effusive Bart. "An ape on the bongo in a band is the most fantastic thing! The band hasn't even spotted Coco in their midst!"

Ash and Josh did their last spins of the tango on the granite tiles. The tango came to an end and Coco ended with a little riff. Still in her feminine dress, she dashed off the stage to Madge and Rod. The clapping was massive and effusive. Madeline, from the hotel staff, told the band that a determined ape had been on the stage with them.

"We had an elusive ape in our band?" said a pensive person from the band. "I cannot comprehend that! That ape is better on the bongo than I am!"

Ash's Medicine

The dinner was definitely one of the best they had had. The tables had jasmine and votive candles on them. Coco was no longer active and had settled in her bassinet under the table for a rest.

"I must take my medicine! I must take the medicine with dinner or the result can be erosive," said Ash.

"That is alarming!" said Josh. "You must definitely take it pronto."

"I am the opposite," said Rod. "I don't take my medicine when I should."

"Rod, you must be more determined than that. Being so passive can be risky. What medicine must you take?" said Madge.

"It is an elective medicine made out of native plants," said Rod.

Josh and Ash Dance

More dancing went on after dinner. They danced the swing and the tango. Josh was determined to dance with Ash as much as possible.

"Josh, I am not being evasive but this dinner dance has been massive for me. I'm not totally well. I need to get some rest at the lodge," admitted Ash.

"You are pale, Ash! I have been selfish. Obviously this is too much for you. I didn't want Bart to dance with you. That was my motive." admitted Josh.

"Silly Josh!" said Ash. "Bart is my boss. I don't want to dance or have a fling with him!" Josh felt glad.

Madge came over. "No more festive fun for me! Let's go to the lodge," said a determined Madge. "I have an angry little ape that must get to bed fast!"

Rod the Baby Ape Daddy

The car's engine made Coco rest and she slept in Rod's arms in a little bundle.
"It is fantastic being an adoptive dad!" said Rod tenderly.
"Isn't it too invasive to have an ape in your life?" said Bart.
"It is a big thing to have an ape. A person must ponder the notion extensively to determine if he is able to live with an ape. It is an infinite task—like having a human baby!" said Rod. "But I love Coco."
"You must go through a lot if you are the dad of a baby ape," said Bart pensively.
"Would you like to adopt an ape, Bart? We do have some critics. Some insist they are not native animals. Some insist they are invasive. But that is not so! I insist the opposite. We used apes in our labs. We must tend and love the lab apes indefinitely and infinitely now that the lab tests are over," said Rod.
"I am a bit smitten with your little Coco!" admitted Bart.

The Smitten Lad

The car went to the nut farm lodge. The smell of jasmine was in the gentle wind. Josh said effusively, "That was the best festive dance I have been to! The band was fantastic, the dinner was splendid, Coco was so engaging, and Ash was the nicest and most feminine person for me to dance with. I wish the dance went on infinitely! I am determined it will happen more."

"It was fantastic. Bless you for that, but I must get Ash off to bed. She is not totally well," Madge said to Josh.

Josh was pensive and went to his cabin. Bart and Ash went off to their beds.

"That lad is smitten. He is effusive in his crush!" said Rod to Madge.

"He is! And that was a massive, festive event!" said Madge as she rested with Coco on the mat.

"It was! I loved being there with you and Coco. Madge, you are a fantastic lass. Will you be ...?" Rod started to ask; but Madge and Coco slept.

LESSON 39

The Nut Farm

"It has been like a vacation here on the nut farm, except for the clinic bit," said Bart. "We must get some work done for the nut farm TV presentation!"

"Right!" said Rod. "I plan to go with Josh's dad to the nut arbors on the farm. He has Doctor Mike Webster here from Oxford to inspect and offer advice on the arbors. Doctor Webster is a world-famous nut farming advisor. It would be worth it for you and Ash to include this in your TV presentation."

"Absolutely! I have a memory of Doctor Mike from a bit on TV on native plants. He is an adept and engaging man," said Bart. "Ash, when we go to the nut farm to make our TV presentation I must bring my visor. The sun is so hot!"

"Will you come with us, Madge?" asked Rod.

"I must take Coco to the vet," said Madge. "She could have ringworm!"

"Oh no!" said Rod in horror. "Humans can get ringworm, too!"

Sam Assists

"There is no Uber in our farming community, but I would love to assist you with this trip," said Sam.

"That is splendid of you, Sam! I do not want to overwork you," said Madge.

"I am glad to assist. Besides, I happen to have a bit of a crush on your Coco," said Sam.

Madge discerned that Sam was an army veteran, too.

"Don't worry about Coco's rash. It is a minor thing," said Sam.

They got to the clinic. The vet's lessor was there to inspect the clinic and he insisted that the vet must inspect it with him.

"The lessor likes to inspect the clinic with fervor. He is a bit of a terror and has no humor. This is so tedious," one of the vet's workers told Madge.

"Tell the lessor that an animal is here for emergency attention!" insisted Sam.

"Sit in the parlor and I will tell him," said the worker.

Coco and the Vet

Doctor Shelly, the vet, was glad to escape the lessor's inspection for a bit. As soon as Doctor Shelly spotted them she said, "Hi Sam! There was a rumor that there was an ape in the community! Come through."

Madge, Sam, and Coco went right through to Doctor Shelly's space for animal patients. Madge put Coco on a bed. "I must inspect Coco over here as I have a dog in labor over there," said Dr Shelly. "Do me a favor and tell me Coco's complete tale!"

"Coco is a happy, adept little ape and has been fine till I spotted some ringworm on her," said Madge.

"Ringworm is a fungus and is infectious!" said Dr Shelly. "Let me inspect it."

Coco giggled and wiggled as Dr Shelly set to work. "Isn't she a marvelous, engaging animal!" said Dr Shelly. "I am happy to tell you that you made an error. It isn't ringworm. It is only a rash—but rasping it will worsen it."

"It isn't a tumor, is it?" said Madge.

"No, it is only a little rash," said Dr Shelly. "You can put this medicine on the rash to help Coco settle. Has she had a pill for worms? I can give her a banana flavor tablet. She will savor that."

An Art Lesson for Coco

Coco savored the banana flavor tablet that the vet gave her and they left.

"It is time for us to motor to the farm," said Sam. "Would you like to stop by a vendor or two, Madge?"

"I would like to go to a market to get Coco some melons and bananas," said Madge.

"I can do that, and I can take you to the local nut factory and to where I worship! I am an art tutor over there," said Sam.

"You do artwork, too? You are a talented man, Sam!" said Madge. "Could you give Coco an art lesson, too? I suspect she has the ability to do that."

Inspect the Engine

Madge, Sam, and Coco motored to the nut farm. A sensor in the engine made an alarm go off in the car. They stopped so Sam could inspect the engine. There was an odd vapor being emitted from the engine. It didn't take much work for Sam to get the car going.

"Sam, you are the best man to be with in the event of engine hassles!" said a happy Madge.

They got back to the lodge in time for dinner.

"My word, Madge! That was a worry! I am glad the worst did not happen!" said Rod. "Has Coco got ringworm?"

"No, I made an error. The vet said it was only a rash and gave her a banana flavor tablet for worms," said Madge. "Was the visit by the arbor doctor from Oxford interesting?"

"Doctor Webster is a marvellous advisor. He gave Josh's dad a lot of nut arbor tips," admitted Rod.

LESSON 40

Melon for Lunch

Chad, the twins' dad, chopped up some melon for their lunch. "Melon again?" lamented Webster.

"Yes, melon again, Webster. Be glad that you have it. Children are hungry in China!" said Chad.

"Have you been to China, Dad? Did you happen to spot hungry children over there?" said Wade.

That made Chad flinch and he said, "No, I have not been there, but that is what Grandpa used to tell me and that made me munch my lunch!"

"Dad, can I make a sandwich?" said Webster.

Wade chimed in, "Are you even able to make a sandwich, Webster?"

"I can do such a thing! I am a lad with much ability!" insisted Webster as he punched Wade on his arm.

Wade split and told Chad that Webster hit him.

Do Not Punch!

Chad told Webster off. "Use your words! Do not punch! You must be a decent chap!" He added, "Can you even make a sandwich?"

"I am the best sandwich maker in the land. It is a cinch!" Webster insisted.

"But you can't even cut a banana!" giggled Wade.

"There was a lesson on YouTube! I can chop like a pro!" insisted Webster.

"Dad, have you got a stretcher? We need one for Webster. He is going to chop his hand by accident. Then we can take him to the hospital!" giggled Wade.

This was too much for Webster and he punched Wade again, this time on his chest.

Chad was mad at Webster for punching Wade and he was mad at Wade for making Webster angry. "It is challenging being a dad!" admitted Chad.

A Sandwich-Making Lesson

Chad gave the twins a sandwich-making lesson.

"Webster, yours is a bit too chunky. It is over an inch!" said Wade.

"Yours has a stench!" said Webster. "It would make me choke!"

Wade snatched Webster's sandwich. As it fell, Wade said, "Catch!" but they couldn't catch it in time and it fell to the tiles in a mess.

"That was an accident!" insisted Wade. "I was only going to take a bite. It was not my intention to smash it."

"I can patch it up," said Webster.

"No! That would be a filthy thing to do!" said Chad. "You two are maddening! Chat nicely! Be chums or I am going to dispatch you to Grandpa!"

Going to Grandpa

"Is going to Grandpa supposed to be a punishment for us?" said Wade. "I like going to Grandpa! He is a champ and lets me hop and have fun with his crutch!"

"Grandpa's crutch is not for fun! It is a medical device to assist him with his sore leg," insisted Chad.

"Grandpa has a little animal from Africa that sits on a perch. Grandpa said it is a terror when it is hungry! It will snatch us if we are bad!" said Webster.

"That is ludicrous!" said Chad. "Grandpa doesn't have such an animal!"

"He does!" insisted Webster. "He said it is invisible!"

"Well, let's chug along to Grandpa's place so that we can visit him and his invisible little animal! Put your things in the hatch," said Chad.

Grandpa the Matchmaker

Chad, Wade, and Webster got to Grandpa's place. Grandpa was happy to see them.

"Fabulous timing, Chad!" said Grandpa. "You can meet Charly!"

"Charly?" the three said.

"Charly is a splendid lass. She makes a fine apple tart, she can dust, and she likes to chat! She has no attachments," said Grandpa.

"Oh no, Dad! Are you being a matchmaker again?" lamented Chad.

"Chad, it is time for a different chapter in your life!" insisted Grandpa. Charly entered the parlor.

"Charly, say hi to Chad. Chad is that rich chap I was pitching to you. I bet he is a match! I chose him for you," said Grandpa.

Chad choked and Charly went red.

"Grandpa!" hissed Wade. "You are in big trouble. Dad is going to be mad!"

Great Job!

*You are ready for the next book,
<u>The Grand Hotel</u>!*

Like this book?

To order additional stories
intended for use with the Learn Reading
program, or to order the full
LEARN READING PROGRAM
Please visit: *LearnReading.com*

Learn Reading is a "real-world" reading acquisition program designed for learners of all ages. It introduces letters and sounds one at a time in the order they appear in everyday English print. Learn Reading also provides comprehensive instruction and opportunity for development in each of the following areas:

- Phonemic awareness
- Decoding
- Sight words
- Vocabulary
- Fluency
- Accuracy and control
- Controlled blending
- Comprehension

Learn Reading integrates several multisensory learning techniques to engage the student and set them up for success. It draws on their prior knowledge, encourages curiosity, and allows them to employ their individual talents to supplement their instruction!

Best of all, the instruction is in video format! The teacher comes to you!

Visit *LearnReading.com* to learn more!

Made in the USA
Middletown, DE
19 July 2024